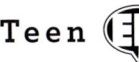 **Teen**

MW01600783

The ELI Readers collection is a
complete range of books and plays
for readers of all ages, ranging from
captivating contemporary stories
to timeless classics. There are three
series, each catering for a different
age group; Young ELI Readers, Teen
ELI Readers and Young Adult ELI
Readers. The books are carefully
edited and beautifully illustrated to
capture the essence of the stories and
plots. The readers are supplemented
with 'Focus on' texts packed with
background cultural information
about the writers and their lives and
times.

ROBERT LOUIS STEVENSON

TREASURE ISLAND

RETOLD AND ACTIVITIES BY SILVANA SARDI
ILLUSTRATED BY BOMBO

Teen ELI Readers

Robert Louis Stevenson
Treasure Island
Retold and activities by Silvana Sardi
Illustrated by Bombo

ELI Readers
Founder and Series Editors
Paola Accattoli, Grazia Ancillani, Daniele Garbuglia (Art Director)

Layout
Gianluca Rocchetti

Production Manager
Francesco Capitano

Photo credits
Shutterstock

© 2012 ELI s.r.l.
P.O. Box 6
62019 Recanati (MC)
Italy
T +39 071750701
F +39 071977851
info@elionline.com
www.elionline.com

Typeset in 13 / 18 pt Monotype Dante

Printed in Italy by Tecnostampa Recanati – ERT223.01
ISBN 978-88-536-0778-2

First edition: February 2012

www.elireaders.com

Contents

These icons indicate the parts of the story that are recorded

Jim Hawkins

Billy Bones

Black Dog

Blind Pew

Dr. Livesey

Squire
TRELAWNEY

LONG JOHN SILVER

CAPTAIN
SMOLLETT

BEN
GUNN

ISRAEL HANDS

Reading

1 **Read the following text and choose the correct word for each space from A, B or C.**

Treasure Island (0)___**A**___ an adventure story. It is (1) _____ a young boy, Jim Hawkins, who (2)_____ friends with (3)_____ old pirate called Billy Bones. From here, (4)_____ adventure begins. There are (5)_____ of strange characters in the story. One of (6)_____ is Long John Silver. He (7)_____ only one leg and a parrot (8)_____ his shoulder. (9)_____ the pirates and Jim's friends want to find the treasure on the (10) _____.

0	**A** is	**B** are	**C** it's
1	**A** from	**B** about	**C** to
2	**A** make	**B** makes	**C** don't make
3	**A** a	**B** one	**C** an
4	**A** her	**B** him	**C** his
5	**A** many	**B** lots	**C** much
6	**A** they	**B** their	**C** them
7	**A** has	**B** haves	**C** have
8	**A** in	**B** on	**C** to
9	**A** between	**B** from	**C** both
10	**A** woods	**B** island	**C** sea

Vocabulary

2 **Match the words that mean the same.**

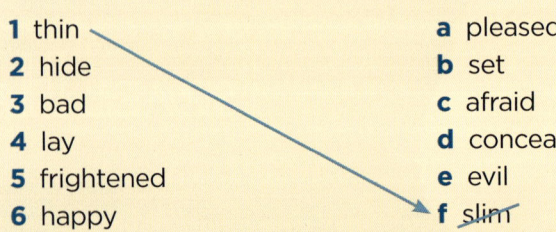

1 thin	**a** pleased
2 hide	**b** set
3 bad	**c** afraid
4 lay	**d** conceal
5 frightened	**e** evil
6 happy	**f** slim

KET – Listening

▶ 2 **3** **Listen to the beginning of chapter 1 and choose the correct answer – A, B or C.**

Jim Hawkins lived with	**A** ☐	an admiral.
	B ☑	his parents.
	C ☐	Ben.

1 His home was
- **A** ☐ near the beach.
- **B** ☐ in south-east England.
- **C** ☐ in a city.

2 The seaman's chest was
- **A** ☐ big and white.
- **B** ☐ big and heavy.
- **C** ☐ big and old.

3 He liked the place because
- **A** ☐ he could drink rum.
- **B** ☐ it wasn't noisy.
- **C** ☐ he liked watching sheep.

4 His telescope was made of
- **A** ☐ brass.
- **B** ☐ gold.
- **C** ☐ silver.

5 In the evening, the seaman
- **A** ☐ never said a word.
- **B** ☐ always asked about someone.
- **C** ☐ chatted to everybody all night.

6 Billy Bones wanted to know about
- **A** ☐ the sea.
- **B** ☐ the weather that day.
- **C** ☐ a seaman.

7 He promised Jim Hawkins
- **A** ☐ lots of gold.
- **B** ☐ a leg of ham.
- **C** ☐ a penny.

Chapter 1

Billy Bones and his Sea Chest

▶ 2   Jim Hawkins lived with his mother and father in an inn* called the 'Admiral Benbow'. It was in a seaside village in south-west England.

One day an old seaman* arrived at the inn with a big heavy chest*. He had a white scar* on his face and looked very fierce.

He drank a glass of rum. Then he asked for a room and said:

'I like it here. It's quiet and I can watch the ships.'

His name was Billy Bones. Every day he looked out to sea through his brass telescope. He didn't speak much, but every night he asked the same question:

'Did any seamen come today?'

One day he called Jim Hawkins and said:

'I will give you a penny my boy if you tell me when a seaman with one leg comes to this inn.'

'Of course!' said Jim, happy to earn a penny. ■

▶ 3   Months passed but no one-legged seaman came.

inn a small hotel
seaman mariner
chest a big container
scar a mark caused by a deep cut

Then, one morning in January, a strange man arrived at the inn.

Jim was laying* the table for breakfast and looked up as the man came in. His face was thin and grey. Then Jim noticed his left hand. He had only three fingers.

'I wonder if Billy Bones will give me my penny for a man with three fingers instead of one leg,' he thought.

'Come here boy,' said the man. 'Tell me, is this Billy Bones' table?'

'Yes,' answered Jim, 'but he's walking on the cliffs* at the moment. You can wait for him here.'

'Good idea boy!' said the man and sat down to wait.

When Billy Bones returned from his walk and saw the man he wasn't very happy.

'Black Dog!' he said. 'What are you doing here?'

'Aren't you pleased* to see an old shipmate*?' asked Black Dog.

Jim left the two men to speak in private. Then there was a loud CRASH! When he went back into the room, Billy Bones was lying on the floor and Black Dog was gone.

Luckily Billy Bones was not dead, but he had to

lay prepare
cliff steep rock by the sea
pleased content
shipmate a sailor

stay in bed for a long time after his fight with his 'old friend' Black Dog.

During this time, Jim cared for the old man and one day Billy said: 'You are always kind to me Jim, so now I'll tell you a secret.'

Jim sat on the bed and listened carefully.

'Do you remember Black Dog?'

'Of course!' answered Jim.

'Well, he's a bad man and there are lots more like* him who want to see me dead!'

'But why?' asked Jim.

'They want my old sea chest. We were all members of Captain Flint's crew*,' he continued.

'Who's Captain Flint?' asked Jim.

'Captain Flint! He was a famous pirate and we had lots of adventures together!'

Jim was so surprised that he couldn't say a word.

'Don't be afraid Jim, my pirate days are over*. But I need your help now. When I die, you mustn't let* the others take my sea chest. Promise!'

'Ok, I promise, but what's inside the sea chest?'

'You'll see when you open it,' was all Billy said.

like similar to
crew group of sailors
over finished
let permit

One afternoon, a blind* man arrived at the inn and asked for Billy Bones. Jim took him to Billy's table. The two men said nothing, but the blind man gave Billy a note* and left quickly.

'Who was that?' asked Jim.

But Billy didn't answer. He looked at the note. His face went very white, then he said:

'Ten o'clock! Quick Jim we have six hours…'

He stood up, then fell to the floor… dead!

Jim stared at the dead man, too shocked to cry.

Then he remembered his promise to Billy.

'The sea chest!' he exclaimed, 'Ten o'clock, six hours!' and he ran upstairs to Billy's room.

The sea chest was under the window. Jim opened it slowly. Inside there were two pistols, an old Spanish watch, a compass and some shells.

Then in the corner of the chest, Jim found a small bag of coins and a long package*. He put everything into a bag and thought:

'I must hide* everything before the blind man and his friends come back.'

So, he took his bag and quietly left the inn.

blind can't see
note short written message
package packet, parcel
hide conceal, keep secret

It was night now and there was a full moon. Jim started to walk to the next village. Just as he reached a bridge, he heard a noise and looked back. Not far behind, he could see some men with lanterns*. They were coming towards him. He thought quickly. Instead of crossing the bridge, he hid under it.

Soon the men arrived at the bridge. One of them was the blind man.

'I can't see the boy anywhere, Pew,' said one of the buccaneers* to the blind man.

'You're not the only one!' exclaimed Pew.

'We must find him. He has the map that was in the chest,' continued Pew. 'Remember, if we find the map, we will be as rich as kings!'

Under the bridge, Jim listened and was scared* and excited at the same time.

Then they heard horses coming from the village. The men ran away and left blind Pew in the middle of the road. The horse hit Pew as it came over the bridge. He died instantly.

The rider*, Doctor Livesey, got off his horse.

Livesey was not only a doctor but also a

lantern light
buccaneer pirate
scared frightened
rider horseman

16

magistrate and Jim knew him well. The doctor took him to his house and Jim told him his story.

'So, Jim,' said the doctor, 'where's the map?'

'Here it is, Sir,' said Jim as he gave the doctor the package. The doctor looked at it for a long time but did not open it. Instead he said:

'You must be hungry Jim. Stay for dinner!'

'Oh thank you Sir,' said Jim.

Mr. Trelawney, the squire*, was also at the dinner and while they ate, the two men told Jim the story of Captain Flint.

'Flint was a terrible pirate. Before dying, he buried* his treasure in a secret place,' they said.

'But now we have the map, thanks to you Jim!' said the doctor.

They opened the package. Inside there was a map of an island with three red crosses* and 'treasure here' written near one of them.

'Right, tomorrow I'm going to buy a ship*,' said the squire, 'and we will sail to the island!'

'And find the treasure!' said the doctor and Jim.

squire a property owner
bury hide under ground
cross X
ship a big boat, vessel

After-reading Activities

Reading

1 **Who are they? Match each description to the right person.**

Jim Hawkins ───────▶ He lives with his parents in an inn

1 Mr. Trelawney   **a** He's a magistrate
2 Billy Bones   **b** He's got only three
                                   fingers on his left hand
3 Black Dog   **c** He's blind
4 Dr. Livesey   **d** He's a squire
5 Pew   **e** He's got a scar on his face

Writing

2 **Complete the questions with a word from the box, then match them to the right answer.**

who	why	~~what~~	where	when	whose

What does Billy Bones promise to give Jim?   **f**

1 .... is Billy Bones' sea chest heavy?   ____
2 .... was Captain Flint?   ____
3 .... does Jim Hawkins hide from Pew and his men? ____
4 .... horse hits Pew?   ____
5 .... does Black Dog arrive at the inn?   ____

a One morning in January.
b Doctor Livesey's.
c He has a lot of things in it.
d A famous pirate.
e Under a bridge.
f ~~A penny.~~

Vocabulary

3 **Find the opposites of the following words in the wordsearch.**

	south	*north*	
1	heavy	....	
2	quiet	....	
3	question	....	
4	thin	....	

5	happy	....
6	something	....
7	upstairs	....
8	slowly	....
9	small	....

```
Y  U  N  Y  S  F  D  L  J  J  C
D  R  E  W  S  N  A  F  D  A  A
D  O  W  N  S  T  A  I  R  S  G
C  E  C  F  B  L  D  A  S  P  E
S  Y  B  A  E  P  A  T  Q  X  H
A  L  I  T  M  Y  J  W  Q  T  T
C  K  G  Y  S  I  O  N  U  U  R
A  C  R  E  T  W  G  Z  R  D  O
Z  I  H  R  C  P  E  Z  X  E  N
O  U  R  L  I  G  H  T  L  J  J
I  Q  G  N  I  H  T  O  N  D  M
```

KET Reading

4 **Read the definitions and complete the words.**

	You drink from this	....	g_l_ _a_s_s_
1	You use this to see far	....	t _ _ _ _ _ _ _ _
2	You put your treasure in this	....	c _ _ _ _
3	You wear a ring on this	....	f _ _ _ _ _
4	An old-fashioned light	....	l _ _ _ _ _ _
5	You find these on the beach	....	s _ _ _ _ _

Chapter 2

The Voyage*

▶ 4 Mr. Trelawney went to Bristol to buy the ship. Jim stayed with Doctor Livesey and dreamt of the mysterious island and the buried treasure.

Many weeks passed, then a letter finally arrived for the doctor:

> *Bristol*
>
> *3rd March*
>
> *Dear Livesey,*
>
> *The ship is ready to start our voyage. Its name is 'Hispaniola'. The people here in Bristol are all very interested in this story about the treasure, and helped me to find the ship.*
>
> *Then I met an old sailor with only one leg. His name is Long John Silver. He will be our cook on board* – poor man he needed a job. Silver also helped me to find the rest of the crew.*
>
> *So, come as fast as you can with Jim, so we can start our adventure.*
>
> *John Trelawney*

voyage journey
on board on the ship

When Jim heard about the man with one leg, he remembered Billy Bones and felt worried, but he said nothing.

Jim and Doctor Livesey left that evening.

They arrived in Bristol next morning and Squire Trelawney was waiting for them at an inn near the docks★. Jim was too excited to eat his breakfast. He sat outside and watched the ships and the sailors at work.

Then the squire told Jim to go to the 'Spy-Glass' inn with a note for John Silver. Jim walked along the docks until he came to Silver's tavern★.

When he entered, he saw a tall man at the bar. The man had only one leg. He was smiling and seemed friendly.

'He doesn't look like an evil★ pirate, not like Black Dog and the blind man Pew,' thought Jim.

'Excuse me Sir,' said Jim. 'Are you Mr. Silver?'

'Yes,' answered the man. 'How can I help you?'

'I have a letter for you from the squire.'

'Ah you must be our new cabin-boy,' said Silver.

dock waterfront
tavern pub
evil bad

21

At that moment, a man at a table near them, stood up and ran out the door.

As he passed, Jim saw his face and cried*:

'Stop him! That's Black Dog!'

'Who?' asked Silver in surprise.

'He's a pirate!'

'A pirate in my tavern! Well, don't worry my boy, you are safe* with me. I won't let him come here again.'

Jim was now completely convinced that Silver was a good man.

'Tell me boy, what is your name?'

'Hawkins Sir, Jim Hawkins.'

'Well, Hawkins,' continued Silver, 'you are a smart* boy. You remembered the face of that pirate. Let's go to Squire Trelawney and tell him the story. I'm sure he'll be happy to hear you are a good boy.'

Jim felt very proud*. He happily walked back along the docks with Silver to the squire.

As they walked, Silver told Jim all about the different ships they could see in the port.

cried shouted
safe free from danger
smart intelligent
proud content

At the inn Silver told the squire and the doctor about Jim and they agreed* he was a smart boy.

When Silver went away, Jim said:

'Squire Trelawney, I think Mr. Silver will be perfect for the voyage.'

'Yes, I like him too,' said the doctor.

'Good!' said the squire. 'Let's go to the ship and see the new captain. His name is Smollett.'

When they boarded the 'Hispaniola', Captain Smollett asked to speak to the squire.

'Sir,' he said, 'I don't like voyages for treasure. They're dangerous, especially when everybody knows about the treasure, the island and the map! And I don't like the crew!'

Doctor Livesey looked at the squire in horror.

'Did you tell everyone about the map too?'

'No, no!' said the squire.

'Well, it doesn't matter* who it was. They know now,' said the doctor.

'You must keep arms* on board,' continued the Captain, 'in case of mutiny*.'

'Mutiny!' said the squire. 'No, impossible! I chose the men myself!'

agree have the same opinion
it doesn't matter it isn't important
arms weapons
mutiny revolt

'Some of the men are honest,' said Captain Smollett, 'but I'm not sure about Silver's men.'

'Well,' said the squire, 'we all think Mr. Silver is a good man, so I'm sure his men are good too.'

'It is your decision,' said Captain Smollett, 'but be careful★.'

'Don't worry Captain Smollett, we aren't stupid,' said the squire.

They spent the rest of the day preparing the ship. Early next morning, they started their voyage to Treasure Island.

The crew worked well and they all respected and obeyed★ Long John Silver, the cook. They called him 'Barbecue'. He was kind★ to everybody, and always had time for Jim.

Silver had a parrot★ and its name was Captain Flint, after the famous pirate.

'Jim, my boy, that parrot is very old and has seen all of the world,' said Silver one day.

Jim loved to hear about Silver's adventures.

Even Captain Smollett started to think that the crew was good and he now loved the ship.

be careful be on guard
obey be loyal to
kind friendly, generous
parrot a colourful, talking bird

The squire was also kind. There was always a barrel* of apples on the ship for the men to eat.

One night, after working hard, Jim decided to have an apple. He saw the barrel and climbed into it, but it was empty*.

Just then, Silver came and sat near the barrel. He started talking to his men. He didn't know Jim was in the barrel listening. Silver and his men were planning to mutiny!

Jim stayed in the barrel, too afraid to move.

'Flint was a great captain,' said Silver to his men, 'and we were the best pirates! We had some accidents, me with my leg, Pew with his eyes, but we had great adventures together. There was always a lot of blood, but lots of gold* too! We will wait until the doctor and the squire take us to the treasure. Then, when it is on board, we will kill those two fools*, Smollett, and that boy Hawkins!'

Inside the barrel, Jim was furious.

'I must tell the squire and Doctor Livesey,' he thought.

barrel cylindrical container
empty containing nothing
gold precious yellow metal
fool stupid person

Then, someone shouted:

'Land ahead*!'

There in front of them was the island. In the confusion, Jim escaped* from the barrel.

He found the doctor and said:

'Come to your cabin with Squire Trelawney and Captain Smollett. I have terrible news!'

In the cabin, Jim told them the whole* story.

'Captain,' said the squire, 'you were right! We have a mutiny!'

'That is not important now,' said Captain Smollett. 'There are three points to consider. First, we must go on*, we can't turn back. Second, we must think of a plan before we find the treasure. Third, there are still some members of the crew who are not part of Silver's group.'

'Counting us and Hawkins, there are seven of us against nineteen of them,' said the doctor.

'Well, we must be positive,' said the squire. 'Silver likes Jim. He can be our spy, so we can organise our attack better.'

Jim promised to do his best to help.

ahead in front
escape get out of
whole complete
go on continue

After-reading Activities

KET-Reading

1 **Choose the correct word (A, B or C) to complete the sentences about chapter 2.**

Mr. Trelawney _went_ to Bristol to buy a ship.

A arrived   **B** went   **C** was

1 The squire _____ Jim to go to the Spy-Glass inn with a note for John Silver.

A said   **B** answered   **C** told

2 Black Dog stood _____ and ran out the door.

A down   **B** up   **C** under

3 Jim was convinced that Silver was a _____ man.

A good   **B** well   **C** best

4 Captain Smollett was worried because _____ knew about the treasure and the map.

A everywhere **B** everything   **C** everybody

5 Early _____ morning they left for Treasure Island

A again   **B** soon   **C** next

6 Jim heard Silver talking about their plans to mutiny and was ____ afraid to move.

A too   **B** much   **C** more

7 There were still _____ men who were not part of Silver's group of pirates

A no   **B** some   **C** any

Grammar

2 **Choose the correct alternative.**

The people in Bristol is / _are_ all interested in the story about the treasure.

1 Jim likes _watch_ / _watching_ the ships in the port.

2 Captain Smollett _doesn't_ / _don't_ like the crew.

3 Captain Smollett _think_ / _thinks_ the voyage is dangerous.

4 Silver and his men are _plan_ / _planning_ to mutiny.

5 Jim _has_ / _have_ terrible news for his friends.

Vocabulary

3a Unscramble these words from chapter 2. Then use each of them once to complete the sentences below.

ereursta   *treasure*

1 trpiea   _____

2 ckods   _____

3 govaye   _____

4 daslin   _____

5 nityum   _____

6 ratpor   _____

3b They all want to find the buried *treasure.*

1 Mr. Silver has a colourful _____.

2 The ships are waiting in the _____.

3 Captain Smollett is worried about _____ on board.

4 It will be a long _____.

5 The _____ is far from Bristol.

6 Captain Flint was a famous _____.

Before-reading Activities

Speaking

4 How do you think Jim and his friends will fight against the pirates?
Discuss with a partner.

Listening

▶ 5   **5** Now listen to the start of chapter 3.
What do they plan to do? Were your ideas similar?

Chapter 3

*Adventure Ashore**

▶ 5 Next morning, they were quite near the island and Jim could see lots of trees. Behind them, there were three hills*.

Jim thought that Treasure Island looked grey and sad. After months at sea, he wasn't even excited about going on land.

The men were all very nervous and nobody wanted to work. The only happy person was Silver. He talked and smiled and worked as usual.

The squire, Doctor Livesey and Captain Smollett had a meeting. Jim was there too.

'Why don't we let the men go ashore for the afternoon?' suggested the Captain.

'Why?' asked the squire.

'Because we can stay on the ship and attack them when they come back!' said the Captain.

'Good idea!' said the doctor.

They also told Hunter, Joyce and Redruth, the only three sailors they could trust*. ◼

ashore on land
hill elevated area
trust depend on

So, Captain Smollett went and spoke to the crew:

'It's a hot day and you are all tired. You can go ashore for the afternoon and relax. I will signal★ when it's time to come back,' he said.

The men all cheered★ and Captain Smollett let Silver decide if anyone had to stay on the ship, or if they could all go ashore.

Finally they were ready. Six men stayed on board, and thirteen including Silver went on land.

With six pirates still on board, they couldn't plan their attack, so Jim decided to go ashore with Silver and the others.

'Maybe I can find the treasure before them,' he thought.

There were two small boats to take them to the island. Jim's boat arrived first. He jumped out and ran into the woods. The last thing he heard was Silver shouting★ from the other boat:

'Jim! Jim! Wait for us!'

Jim ran and ran until he felt safe. Then he started to explore the island. There were lots of trees, plants and flowers.

signal indicate
cheer say hurrah
shout call loudly

While he was walking, he suddenly* heard somebody nearby. He quickly hid behind some plants.

It was Silver and his men. They were very near.

Suddenly there was a horrible scream*, then another, then silence.

'Well that's the end of Tom and Alan,' said Silver.

Through the trees, Jim saw him cleaning his knife on his trousers. The knife was red with blood.

'Oh no!' he thought. 'Poor Tom and Alan are dead!'

'Is there anyone else* who doesn't want to be a pirate and follow me?' asked Silver.

Nobody answered.

'Good then,' he said. 'Now we only need to find the boy.'

Jim trembled* with fear on hearing his name.

He waited until Silver and his men started walking again. Then he ran in the opposite direction.

Jim ran until he reached a hill. He stopped for a moment. Suddenly something moved behind the tree in front of him. He didn't know if it was a person or an animal.

suddenly unexpectedly
scream cry
else more, other
tremble shake

Jim decided to return to the boats, but this strange creature followed him. Now he could see it was a man.

'Maybe he's a cannibal!' thought Jim and reached for his gun*.

Jim pointed the gun at the man and said:

'Who are you?'

'Ben Gunn,' said the man. 'Please don't shoot me. I only want to talk to you. The last time I spoke to someone was three years ago.'

'Three years?' asked Jim.

'Yes, I was marooned* here three years ago.'

Jim knew this was how pirates punished their men.

'Did pirates leave you to die on this deserted island?'

'Yes,' said Ben Gunn, 'but I'm not dead yet, and I know all the secrets of this island.'

They sat down and Ben Gunn said:

'Life is hard on this island. I look like* a beggar* with my old clothes but really I'm rich.'

gun pistol
marooned abandoned
look like seem
beggar vagabond

34

'Rich?' said Jim.

'Yes, my boy. And you will be rich too!'

'I don't understand,' said Jim. 'All I want is to return to my ship, but I can't.'

'Why can't you go back?' asked Ben Gunn.

'Because Silver will kill me,' said Jim

'Not Silver, the man with one leg?' asked Ben.

'Yes, Long John Silver. He's the cook on board and the leader of the other pirates.'

'I know him,' said Ben Gunn. 'He's evil.'

Jim told Ben Gunn about their voyage and the problems they now had with the pirates.

'I will help you, but the squire must help me too,' said Ben Gunn. 'Tell him I want £1000 and a ship to take me home. In return*, I will give him some important information.'

'I'm sure the squire will agree,' said Jim

'Good!' said Ben Gunn. 'Now, listen to my story. I was on Captain Flint's ship when he buried the treasure. He went ashore with six men but came back alone*. The others were all dead!'

in return in exchange
alone by oneself

'Oh no!' said Jim. 'Did he kill his own men?'

'Yes,' continued Ben Gunn. 'At that time Billy Bones and Long John Silver were part of the crew. They asked Flint where the treasure was, but he didn't tell them. Then, three years ago, I returned to the island on another ship. I told my shipmates about Flint's treasure. We went ashore and looked for the treasure for twelve days, but we couldn't find it. The crew was angry with me, so they left me on the island. Tell your squire this story Jim. In three years, a man can do a lot of digging★. Tell him that I am a good man.'

'I'm sure you are,' said Jim, 'and I'd love to tell the squire, but how can I return to the ship?'

'I have a boat Jim, you can use it,' said Ben.

Just then, there was the sound of cannon★ fire.

'Oh no!' said Jim, 'they are fighting on the ship. I must go and help my friends!'

'Let's take a shortcut★ through the woods,' said Ben Gunn.

dig excavate
cannon large gun
shortcut faster route

Jim ran fast and cannon balls landed around him. The pirates were firing from the Hispaniola.

Jim stopped to look back at the ship.

'Oh no! The pirate's flag is on the ship,' he said.

Then he saw another flag above the trees in front of him: the Union Jack⋆!

'Look at that flag Ben,' said Jim.

'There is a stockade⋆ in the woods Jim. Your friends must be there,' said Ben. 'Go and see. My boat is under the white rock if you need it. Remember, tell the squire and the doctor that I have important information for them about the treasure.'

'Right, I will,' said Jim and he went in the direction of the flag.

The pirates fired more cannon balls from the ship. Then they burnt⋆ the doctor's small boat. ◼

Union Jack British flag
stockade enclosed area with barrier
burn set on fire

KET-Writing

1 Read this note from Jim's mum.

My Dear Son,
How are you? I am very worried about you.
Are all the crew members nice? I didn't like that man with
the parrot!
Can you see the island yet? I hope you find the treasure
and come home soon.

> Take care.
> love
> *Mum x x*

Imagine you are Jim. Answer his mum's questions in a short
note. Write 25-35 words.

_____

_____

_____

_____

_____

Vocabulary

2 Complete the sentences with one word from the box.

> ashore ~~flag~~ woods trust island wait board

Jim sees the pirate's *flag* flying on the ship.

1 Captain Smollett doesn't _____ Long John Silver.
2 Jim decides to go _____ to look for the treasure.
3 Jim doesn't_____ for the pirates.
4 Life on the_____ is hard.
5 There are a lot of trees in the _____.
6 Some of the pirates stay on _____.

Grammar

3 Choose the correct alternative.

The men are nervous and nobody is *wanting* / *wants* to work.

1 Jim is on the boat now and *he goes* / *is going* ashore with the pirates.
2 While Jim is *walking* / *walks* in the woods, he hears a scream.
3 Jim is *needing* / *needs* help to escape from the pirates.
4 The pirates always are *listening* / *listen* to their leader.
5 Ben Gunn is *knowing* / *knows* the island well.
6 Ben Gunn is *having* / *has* a boat Jim can use.

Speaking

4 Decipher the code and discover what Long John Silver is making his men for dinner.

♠=A ♣=B ♥=C ▫=D ♦=E ■=F ○=G ▲=H ☼=I
◊=J √=K ◀=L ☺=M ♩=N ▼=O ♫=P ▢=Q ☻=R
Ω=S ±=T ¤=U §=V ◙=W ▶=X ⌂=Y ∞=Z

■ ☻♦ Ω ▲ ◀⌂   ■☺☼♦ ▫   ■☻♦Ω▲   ■ ☼ Ω ▲

— — — — — — —   — — — — —   — — — — —   — — — —

Before-reading Activity

Listening

▶ 7 **5 Listen to the beginning of chapter 4 and tick True (T) or False (F).**

	T	F
Jim stayed in the woods until morning.	☐	☑
1 The pirates continued fighting all night.	☐	☐
2 Ben's boat was at the stockade.	☐	☐
3 Jim wants to swim back to the ship.	☐	☐
4 The Doctor doesn't know about his boat yet.	☐	☐
5 The Squire opened the door to Jim.	☐	☐

Chapter 4

The Stockade

▶ 7 Jim hid in the woods and waited until it was night. He could see the Hispaniola still anchored* in the same place, but with the Jolly Roger*.

The pirates stopped their attack and started to drink rum. It was quiet now and Jim made for* the stockade.

In the distance, he could see the white rock where Benn Gunn kept his boat.

'I must remember that rock,' thought Jim. 'We will need a boat to return to our ship. The doctor won't be happy when I tell him what the pirates did to his boat.'

At last he reached the stockade and knocked at the door.

'Doctor! Squire! Captain! It's Jim!'

The Doctor opened the door and exclaimed:

'Jim, my boy! You are alive!'

'Oh Doctor, it's good to see you!'

■

anchor secure a ship
Jolly Roger pirate's flag
make for go in the direction of

8   'How did you get here?' asked Jim.

'Come in my boy, and I'll tell you about our adventure.'

Everyone was happy to see Jim again. They sat at the table and the doctor began:

'Well, we realised that you were on the island Jim. We wanted to know if you were alright, so Hunter and I came ashore. After walking for a long time, we found this stockade. As you can see, it's in a fantastic position. There is fresh water and it gives great protection. Suddenly, I heard a terrible scream. I thought it was you Jim.'

'No, doctor, I heard that scream too, it was Tom and Alan,' said Jim.

'Are they both dead?'

'Yes, Long John Silver killed* them,' said Jim.

'The scoundrel*!' said the doctor.

'Well, after that scream,' continued the doctor, 'I decided to return to the ship for the others because the stockade was safer.'

kill murder
scoundrel villain

'I can't believe we are all safe,' said Jim. 'How did you do it?'

'Well,' said the doctor, 'it wasn't easy but we made a plan. First, we put food, medicine and arms in a small boat.'

'What about Silver's six men?' asked Jim. 'How did you escape from them?'

'They were no problem,' said the doctor. 'The squire and Captain Smollett gave them lots of rum. Then, the Captain threatened* to shoot them if they didn't stay in their cabins. The pirates were so drunk* that they didn't object*. Some of them even slept! When the boat was full, three of us brought the things to the stockade. I left these two men at the stockade, then I returned to the Hispaniola for the squire, Redruth and Captain Smollett. This time the sea was not very calm. The current was very strong and we couldn't reach the stockade from our position. We had to do something fast, before the pirates saw us.'

'What did you do?' asked Jim.

threaten warn
drunk intoxicated by alcohol
object say no

'Well we tried to row⋆ faster, but it was very difficult. Then I looked back at the Hispaniola and there on the top deck were Silver's men with the cannon!' They were aiming⋆ it at us! Squire Trelawney tried to shoot one of them but he missed⋆. Then the other pirates on shore boarded⋆ one of their boats and started to come towards us.'

'Oh no!' said Jim. 'Pirates everywhere!'

'Yes, but we were lucky Jim. A big wave⋆ took us onto the shore. At that moment the cannon ball passed over our heads and fell in the water nearby!'

'You must have been scared,' said Jim. 'Did you get hurt?'

'No, no. We went ashore, leaving our things in the boat,' said the doctor.

'The problem was, we only had two guns. We could hear the pirates coming near. We ran as fast as we could towards the stockade and got here just before the pirates reached us.'

'But who had the Union Jack?' asked Jim.

'That was Captain Smollett. His jacket was full

row move boat with oar   **board** embark
aim point   **wave** crest
miss not hit target

of stuff*. When we arrived, he went out and put the flag up.'

'That was lucky for me,' said Jim. 'I saw the flag and found you!'

'Yes, but it was also a help to Silver's men,' said the doctor. 'The pirates on the ship attacked us with cannon balls. They aimed at the flag. We couldn't go out and get our things from our boat. Luckily the cannon balls didn't hit* anybody, but those greedy* pirates took all our supplies*. We couldn't move from here.'

'So is there no food now?' asked Jim. He was thinking about Ben Gunn.

'Well there is some, but we must be very careful,' answered the doctor. 'Are you hungry my boy? You can eat something if you want.'

'No, no,' said Jim. 'I'm too excited to eat!'

'Well Jim, tell us about your adventure now,' said the doctor.

Jim told them about his adventure ashore. He also spoke about Ben Gunn.

stuff things
hit reach with shot
greedy avid/selfish
supplies provisions, food

'Once we solve the problem with the pirates, we will speak to Ben Gunn,' said the squire.

The doctor made meat for dinner. Then they sat and talked about their plans.

'Well,' said the Captain, 'I think the only solution is to kill the buccaneers. Now there are only fifteen of them. We have the advantage that they drink too much, so we can beat* them.'

'Also the conditions on the island are bad,' said the doctor. 'They are sleeping in the marsh* and will get cold. We are stronger!'

They went to bed tired but optimistic.

Next morning Jim heard: 'Flag of Truce*!'

'It's Silver with the flag!' said the Captain.

'Captain,' said Silver, 'I want to talk.'

'Well come in,' said the doctor.

Silver entered and sat down at the table.

'Well, gentlemen,' said Silver. 'We want the treasure and the map you have.'

'Ah, is that all?' asked the Captain sarcastically.

'Yes,' said Silver. 'Give us the map and we will not harm* you.'

beat be victorious
marsh wet land
Flag of Truce white flag of surrender
harm hurt

46

'Well, listen to me Silver,' said the Captain.

'We are not scared of you and your men. They are always drunk. They can't fight well and they can't sail* the ship. You will never get the map!'

'Wait and see,' said Silver. 'In an hour you will regret* your words!'

With these words, he went back to his pirates. The Captain and the others in the stockade prepared for Silver's attack.

'There are more of them,' said the Captain, 'but we have the protection of the stockade.'

An hour passed but there was no sign* of the pirates. Now it was sunny and very hot.

Then suddenly, a group of pirates came out of the woods. They ran towards the stockade. They started to climb the walls of the stockade. The squire hit three of them. Four ran towards the house, but Captain Smollett and his men fought hard and in the end they won. Five pirates were dead and the others ran back to the woods.

sail navigate
regret be sorry for
sign trace

KET-Reading

1 **Choose A, B or C to complete the conversations.**

I'm afraid of pirates.

A ☐ Neither do I.
B ☐ I'm afraid not.
C ☑ So am I.

1 How big is the island?

A ☐ Quiet, I think.
B ☐ I don't know.
C ☐ About 3 years.

2 What was the stockade like?

A ☐ Yes, they liked it.
B ☐ It was fantastic.
C ☐ No, they didn't.

3 We swam to the shore.

A ☐ Are you?
B ☐ Was the sea calm?
C ☐ We don't.

4 I'm sorry about your boat.

A ☐ Certainly not!
B ☐ If you want.
C ☐ It doesn't matter.

5 Who put the flag up?

A ☐ The Union Jack.
B ☐ Upstairs.
C ☐ The Captain.

6 We must be very careful.

A ☐ Yes, we care.
B ☐ You're right.
C ☐ We do.

Vocabulary

2 Circle the odd word out.

A boat	**B** ferry	**C** train	**D** ship
1 A island	**B** sea	**C** river	**D** lake
2 A jacket	**B** shoes	**C** shirt	**D** jumper
3 A meat	**B** fish	**C** bread	**D** water
4 A clock	**B** minute	**C** second	**D** hour
5 A house	**B** castle	**C** wood	**D** palace
6 A sailor	**B** doctor	**C** magistrate	**D** cannon

Writing

3 Imagine you are Silver. You want to meet the Doctor to talk about the treasure. Write the Doctor a note.

Tell him:

- where to meet.
- what to bring to the meeting.
- who to come with.
Write 25-35 words.

Before-reading Activity

Speaking

4 At the end of this chapter Jim and his friends win against the pirates. What do you think will happen now? Discuss the following questions with your partner. Then read Chapter 5 and check your answers.

1 How many pirates are left?
2 Will the Doctor try to speak to Silver again?
3 Will Jim reach the ship? How?
4 Will the pirates attack again?

Chapter 5

Jim's Adventure at Sea

▶ 9 During the attack on the stockade, Captain Smollett broke his arm. He also lost some men. Now there were four of them left* and eight pirates.

The pirates didn't come back that day and Jim and the others ate quietly inside the stockade.

After lunch, the doctor spoke to the squire and the Captain. Then he took the map and his pistol and went into the woods. He was going to see Ben Gunn.

At the same time Jim Hawkins decided he didn't want to stay in the stockade. It was so hot. He wanted to be in the cool* woods and he wanted some adventure.

He took some biscuits and two pistols and left the stockade. The squire was helping the Captain and didn't see Jim go.

He wanted to go to the white rock where Ben Gunn had his boat.

left remaining
cool fresh

Treasure Island

It was now late afternoon. Jim went through the trees until he came to the sea. The sea was never calm around Treasure Island and the waves crashed against the rocks.

In the distance Jim could see the Hispaniola with the Jolly Roger. The white rock was still far down the coast.

It was dark when Jim finally reached the rock.

Under the rock there was a small cave★. Ben Gunn's boat was there! It was very small and also very light.

Jim decided to use the boat to reach the Hispaniola. He wanted to cut the ship's anchor and let the Hispaniola float★ ashore, so the pirates couldn't leave the island.

He put the boat in the water and rowed in the direction of the ship. It was foggy. The only light Jim could see was from the cabin on the ship.

The waves pushed him towards the side of the ship. Jim found the rope★ of the anchor and cut it.

The pirates on the ship didn't see him.

Jim could hear two pirates in the cabin. They were

cave grotto
float drift
rope cord

drunk and they were shouting. They seemed very angry. Jim stood up in his boat and looked through the cabin window. The two pirates were fighting*.

Suddenly the wind caught the ship and it turned towards the open sea. Jim couldn't control his little boat. It followed the Hispaniola and the waves got bigger and bigger.

Jim lay in the bottom of the boat. The waves crashed around him. He thought he was going to drown*.

He closed his eyes. The waves rocked* the boat and in the end Jim fell asleep. He dreamt of his family and his home, the old 'Admiral Benbow' inn.

Jim woke up early next morning. He was at the south end of Treasure Island and the sun was behind the highest hill on the island.

Jim was near the shore, but on this side of the island there were lots of rocks. He decided to row north where there was soft sand.

The waves carried* the little boat north. The sun was high in the sky. Jim was hot and very thirsty.

fight have a physical dispute
drown go under water and die
rock move back and forward
carry transport

The shore was still quite far. He looked out to sea and saw the Hispaniola. The ship seemed out of control. It moved first in one direction, then in another.

'Those two pirates are probably still drunk,' thought Jim. 'Or maybe there is nobody on the ship now!'

Jim decided to go and see.

'I can give the Hispaniola back to Captain Smollett,' he thought.

He turned his little boat in the direction of the Hispaniola and began to row hard.

Fortunately it wasn't very windy. Jim reached the ship. There were no pirates on deck.

'Maybe they are in the cabin,' thought Jim.

Then a big wave arrived and lifted* Jim's small boat high in the air. The Hispaniola was right next to him. He jumped and landed on the deck of the ship. His little boat broke under the waves.

Now he was stranded* on the Hispaniola.

Jim heard a moan*. Israel Hands, one of Silver's men was lying on the deck next to another dead pirate. His leg was cut badly. He looked at Jim.

lift raise
stranded marooned
moan cry, lament

54

'Brandy,' he said.

The man's face was very white. Jim went down to the cabin for the brandy. The cabin was a disaster. Everything was broken. There were lots of empty bottles.

Finally, Jim found some brandy in a small bottle. He also found some biscuits and water.

Back on deck, he ate and drank. Then he gave the pirate his brandy.

Israel Hands took a long drink and said:

'I needed that boy! How did you get here?'

'I am your captain now, Mr. Hands,' said Jim.

Israel Hands watched as Jim threw the Jolly Roger into the sea, then said:

'Captain Hawkins, do you want to go ashore? Give me some food and a bandage★ for my leg and I will help you sail the ship,' said the pirate.

'It's a deal★,' said Jim.

So they sailed the ship towards the beach in the north.

When they were near the North Inlet★, they had to wait for high tide★.

bandage covering for a cut
deal agreement, pact

inlet bay
high tide high water

ROBERT LOUIS STEVENSON

'Captain Hawkins,' said Israel Hands, 'my leg is very sore*. Can you get me some wine?'

Jim realised the pirate had a plan, but said:

'Of course. I'll go down to the cabin.'

Jim watched the pirate from the stairs. Israel Hands stood up and went to the dead pirate. He took a knife and a rope, then sat down again.

'So he can move and now he's got a knife,' thought Jim. 'I must be careful.'

Jim brought the pirate the wine.

'Thanks Captain,' said Hands. 'Now the tide is right to enter the bay.'

Jim followed Hands' instructions and slowly brought the ship near the shore. Jim concentrated on the manoeuvre, but luckily he turned and saw Hands with the knife.

Hands came towards Jim. The boy moved quickly and took out his pistol.

The pirate threw the knife at Jim's shoulder. Jim squeezed* the trigger* in pain.

There was a shot. Israel Hands fell into the water, dead!

sore painful   trigger part of gun
squeeze put pressure on

Jim looked at the dead man and felt sick* with terror. He pulled the knife from his shoulder. The cut wasn't too deep and he put a bandage on it.

Then he threw the other dead pirate into the water next to Israel Hands.

Now Jim was the only person on the ship. It was night. The front of the Hispaniola lay on the sandy seabed*. Jim jumped off the ship into the shallow* water of the bay.

Once ashore, Jim went quickly towards the stockade. He wanted to tell the others that the ship was waiting for them.

When he reached the stockade, Jim climbed over the wall and crept* to the house. He opened the door and entered. Then he heard:

'Pieces of eight! Pieces of eight!' again and again. It was Silver's parrot, Captain Flint!

'Who goes there?' asked Silver.

Jim realised too late that he was trapped*. The pirates were in possession of the house! ■

sick nauseated
seabed bottom of the sea
shallow not deep

creep (crept) approach unnoticed
trapped captured

After-reading Activities

KET-Reading

1 Read the text and choose a word from A, B or C for each space.

When the doctor went (0) **A** see Ben, he took the map with (1)____. Jim didn't stay (2) ____ the stockade. He wanted to reach Ben Gunn's boat. He found (3)____ in a cave. He rowed (4)____ the Hispaniola, but the waves were very (5)____ and he lost control of (6)____ boat. When he woke (7)____ morning, the sun was behind the (8) ____ hill on the island.

0	**A** ~~to~~	**B** at	**C** in
1	**A** it	**B** him	**C** her
2	**A** for	**B** on	**C** at
3	**A** you	**B** it	**C** them
4	**A** towards	**B** under	**C** between
5	**A** bigger	**B** big	**C** the biggest
6	**A** your	**B** him	**C** his
7	**A** last	**B** next	**C** after
8	**A** higher	**B** more high	**C** highest

Grammar

2 Complete the sentences with a word or expression from the box.

some	very	much	~~many~~	few	lots of

How *many* pirates were there on the ship?
1 There wasn't _____ light, so it was difficult to see.
2 The pirates were drinking _____ beer and there were bottles everywhere.
3 _____ people knew about the cave, only Ben and Jim.
4 Jim was _____ hot and thirsty.
5 He found _____ water on the ship, just a small bottle.

58

Writing

3 **While Jim is sleeping, he dreams about his mother. Complete the conversation he has with her in his dream, with a question (A-E).**

Mother: *(E) Are you alright?*   **Jim:** I'm really tired.

Mother: (1)...............................?
Jim: I can't. The pirates have the ship.
Mother: (2)...................................?
Jim: There are only two left on the ship.
Mother: (3)...................................?
Jim: No, they are too drunk to fight.
Mother: (4)...?
Jim: Yes of course mum.

A How many pirates are there?
B Isn't it too dangerous for you?
C Will you be careful?
D Why don't you come home?
E Are you alright?

Before-reading Activity

Listening

▶ 10 **4** **Listen to the beginning of chapter 6 and tick (✓) True (T) or False (F).**

		T	F
	There were still six buccaneers.	✓	☐
1	The pirates were with Jim's friends.	☐	☐
2	Silver invited Jim to stay with them.	☐	☐
3	Doctor Livesey showed Silver the Hispaniola.	☐	☐
4	Silver and the Doctor decided to stop fighting.	☐	☐
5	The Doctor gave the ship to the pirates.	☐	☐

Chapter 6

The Treasure Hunt

▶ 10 There were six buccaneers left. Jim looked around but couldn't see his friends. The parrot was sitting on Silver's shoulder.

'Well look who it is! Jim Hawkins!' said Silver.

'You know Jim, Captain Smollett and your friends are all angry with you because you left them. Why don't you stay with us?' said Silver.

'So they are still alive,' thought Jim.

'So, my boy, what do you say? Do you want to join* us?' asked Silver.

'First tell me what happened,' said Jim.

'Well, yesterday morning, Doctor Livesey came to us with a flag of truce and said:

'Captain Silver, look out to sea, the Hispaniola is not there!'

'And it was true!' said Silver. 'Then Livesey sat down with me. We talked and we agreed to stop fighting. In return for their freedom*, they gave us this house, food and brandy.'

■

join follow, become part of
freedom liberty

'Where are they now?' asked Jim.

'No idea,' answered Silver, 'and they weren't interested in you Jim.'

'I don't care★,' said Jim. 'I will never become a pirate! You have no ship, no treasure and few men! You can kill me or spare★ me. If you spare me, I will speak well of you in court when they catch you for piracy.'

'Let's kill him now!' shouted the pirates.

'Wait!' ordered Silver. 'I am your Captain. You will not harm the boy, do you understand?'

The other pirates said nothing but they were not pleased with this order. They walked out of the house in disgust and left Jim and Silver alone.

'You're a smart boy Jim,' said Silver. 'I will protect you from my men, and you will save me from the gallows★ if the authorities catch me.'

'I promise,' said Jim.

'I know you have the ship Jim. One thing I don't understand is why the doctor gave me the map.'

'What?' said Jim in surprise.

'Yes, it seems strange to me too,' said Silver.

At last the five pirates came back into the house.

I don't care it isn't important
spare save life
gallows place for execution by hanging

'Captain Silver, we think it's time for a new captain,' said one of the pirates.

'Well, and why is that?' asked Silver.

'First, this voyage is a disaster. Second, you let the enemy* leave this house. Third, you won't let us kill this boy,' said the pirate.

'Well,' said Silver, 'you have a short memory. You wanted to mutiny before we got the treasure on board, I didn't! Number two. I let the enemy go, so we could have food and drink and also because they gave me the map,' continued Silver. 'And the boy? Well he will be a good hostage*!'

Silver pulled out the map for the five pirates to see. At first they said nothing. Then they started to shout and laugh at the same time. They passed the map around, so they could all see it.

Silver sat with his wooden leg on the table and waited for his men to calm down. Jim stood against the wall. He wondered* what the doctor's plan was.

'Now I am ready to resign*,' said Silver.

'No, no,' said the pirates. 'You are our captain!'

'Thank you men for your loyalty*,' said Silver.

enemy adversary
hostage prisoner
wonder ask yourself

resign give up responsibility
loyalty allegiance

Only Jim noticed Silver's sarcasm.

Next morning Jim woke up to a familiar voice.

Silver was speaking to Doctor Livesey.

'Please, come in Doctor. We have some patients* for you and a surprise visitor!'

'Not Jim Hawkins?' asked the doctor.

'Yes,' said Silver.

The doctor stopped for a moment then said:

'Well, first the patients.' He looked at Jim, but said nothing.

He examined all his patients and gave them some medicine. Then he said:

'Now I'd like to speak to Jim please.'

'Well, Doctor,' said Silver. 'If you go outside the stockade, you can speak to Jim through* the hole in the wall.'

The pirates protested but Silver said:

'Thanks to the doctor, we have the map. Let him speak to the boy.'

Silver walked with Jim to the stockade wall. The doctor was waiting on the other side*.

'Doctor,' said Silver, 'don't forget how I am

patient sick person
through by means of, using
side part

64

helping you and the boy now. Remember my good points and save me from the gallows in the future if necessary.'

Silver left the doctor and Jim to speak.

'Doctor, I have the ship,' said Jim.

'The ship!' said the doctor.

'Yes, it's on the north beach.'

Jim told the doctor about his adventure at sea.

'Jim, how can we thank you?' asked the doctor.

'First you discovered the plan to mutiny. Then you met Ben Gunn, now the ship!'

Then the doctor called Silver:

'Silver, be careful on the treasure hunt. I promise that if we both survive* this adventure, I will defend you in court*.'

'Thank you Doctor,' said Silver.

'Remember, always keep the boy near you Silver,' said the doctor. 'We will be there to help you if necessary,' he promised as he left them.

Silver and Jim returned to the other pirates and had breakfast. While they ate, Silver spoke to his men:

'Well, the doctor knows where the ship is. After

survive live through
court building for legal proceedings

we find the treasure, we'll look for it. While we are looking for the treasure, I'll keep our hostage tied* to me. The doctor won't attack us if we have the boy. We'll keep him with us until we have the treasure and are sailing away from this island.'

His men were all happy with this idea. Jim sat in silence. He didn't know if Silver meant* what he said or not.

After breakfast they left the stockade to look for the treasure. They walked through the woods in a line. Silver was first with his parrot on his shoulder. Behind him was Jim with a rope around his waist*. Silver held the other end*. Then the other pirates followed.

They studied the map. The first thing to find was a 'tall' tree, but there were a lot of them. They started to climb up to a plateau*.

Suddenly, a pirate shouted:

'Come here! There's a skeleton under a tree!'

The skeleton was pointing* east.

'Look!' said Silver. 'This must be one of the men Captain Flint killed. The skeleton is showing us where the treasure is. Let's go!'

tie attach, link	**end** extremity
mean have in mind, intend	**plateau** high flat piece of land
waist middle	**point** indicate

66

Then they heard a ghostly* voice singing:
'Fifteen men on the dead man's chest-
Yo-ho-ho, and a bottle of rum!'
The pirates were terrified! They were sure Flint's ghost was coming for them.

'That's no spirit!' said Silver. 'It doesn't even sound like* Flint. It sounds like… of course! It's Ben Gunn!' said Silver.

The pirates were happier now. They weren't afraid of Ben Gunn. They started to walk again.

They were now near the highest hill on the island. At the top under a tree, there was an empty hole*! The treasure was gone! The pirates were furious. They were about to attack Silver and Jim, when three shots came from the woods. Two pirates were hit. The other three ran away.

Then the doctor and Ben Gunn appeared.

'Thank you doctor. You saved our lives,' said Silver. 'But what happened to the treasure?'

'Well,' said the doctor, 'Ben Gunn found it!'

'And where is it now Ben?' asked Silver.

ghostly phantom, supernatural
sound like be similar to
hole cavity, hollow

Treasure Island

'In my cave. I moved it there,' said Ben. 'The squire is watching it for us.'

'Now I understand why you gave the pirates the map, doctor,' said Jim. 'You didn't need it.'

They reached the pirate's small boat and used it to get near* Ben's cave. The squire was waiting for them with the treasure and Captain Smollett. They put the gold in the small boat, then rowed to the Hispaniola.

Silver and Ben Gunn came with them. They left the other three pirates on the island.

They stopped at a port in South America to look for a new crew. Silver took his chance* of freedom. He stole some gold and disappeared*.

The others didn't mind. Their adventure was over. At last they were going home, alive and well, and with the treasure!

get near approach, arrive
chance opportunity
disappear leave no trace

After-reading Activities

KET-Reading

1 Match the sentence halves using a word from the box.

and (2) so but ~~but~~ because when

Jim looked around ....*but*.... he couldn't see his friends.

1 The pirates were not .... **a** they heard the ghost.
pleased with Silver

2 Silver freed Doctor .... **b** a surprise visitor
Livesey   for the doctor.

3 Captain Smollett was .... **c** agreed to stop
angry   fighting.

4 Silver and the Doctor .... **d** his men could have
talked   food and drink.

5 There were some .... **e** they said nothing.
patients

6 The pirates were .... **f** Jim left them.
scared

Grammar

2 Complete the sentences with the correct comparative or superlative form of the adjective in brackets.

Jim was the *youngest* (young) of the crew.

1 Silver was .... (smart) than his men.

2 The pirates were .... (happy) once they saw the map.

3 Captain Flint was the .... (fierce) pirate in the world.

4 They had to climb the .... (high) hill on the island.

5 Captain Smollett was the .... (good) captain in the world.

6 Jim was much .... (brave) than other boys of his age.

7 This was the .... (exciting) adventure a boy could dream of.

Writing

3 **Put the words in the correct order to make questions, then match them to the answers below.**

pirates/ many / left / there / how / were?
How many pirates were there left?
....

1 Silver's / where / parrot / sitting / was?
2 Doctor / flag / when / the / did / with / come / the?
3 Livesey / to / give / the / who / map / did?
4 cave / who / treasure / the / in / hid / the?
5 breakfast / Silver / did / who / with / have?
6 Jim / around / what / waist / have / his / did?
7 use / a / did / small / why / boat / they?

a Ben Gunn. **b** to reach Ben's cave. **c** on his shoulder.
d Silver.   **e** yesterday morning. **f** his men.
g a rope.   **z** ~~six.~~

Vocabulary

4 **Complete the sentences with a word from the box.**

mutiny	~~treasure~~	plateau	hostage
patients	gallows	hole	

They went home with the *t r e a s u r e*.

1 Silver wanted to keep Jim as a _ _ _ _ _ _ _.
2 The Doctor promised to save Silver from the _ _ _ _ _ _ _.
3 The pirates climbed up to a _ _ _ _ _ _ _.
4 There was nothing, only an empty _ _ _ _.
5 Jim discovered the pirates' plan to _ _ _ _ _ _.
6 The Doctor always looked after his _ _ _ _ _ _ _ _.

Robert Louis Stevenson

Biography

Robert Louis Stevenson was born in Edinburgh, the capital of Scotland on November 13th 1850. His father Thomas was Scottish and was an expert at building lighthouses. His mother Margaret Isabella was French and was gentle and full of fun. As a child Robert was very thin and often ill, so he spent a lot of time in France where the weather was better than in Scotland. He was an only child and from an early age loved listening to the adventure stories his nurse told him at bedtime.

Early Works

After school, he went to Edinburgh University to become an engineer like his father. However he did not like these studies. He was more interested in literature and started to write for the university magazine. His first book *An Inland Voyage* about travelling in France, was published in 1878. He loved travelling, and during one of his trips he met and fell in love with an American woman, Fanny Vandegrift. He went to the USA with Fanny and they got married in San Francisco in 1880. This journey gave him a lot of ideas for his future books.

Robert Louis Stevenson, 1885

Photograph of Robert Louis Stevenson and family, on the island of Upolu in Samoa.

The Successful Writer

He returned to Europe where he became a popular writer with the publication of Treasure Island.

Apart from this adventure novel, two of his most famous works are *Kidnapped* and *The Strange Case of Dr. Jekyll and Mr. Hyde*. After his father died in 1887, he returned to the USA, where he was now famous too.

Then, during a cruise of the islands in the Pacific, he discovered that the climate in this part of the world was very good for his health. He decided to move with his family to Upolu, the main island of Samoa in the Pacific Ocean. He lived happily there with his family and continued to write until he died in 1896. The local people loved him and called him 'Tusitala' which means 'storyteller'.

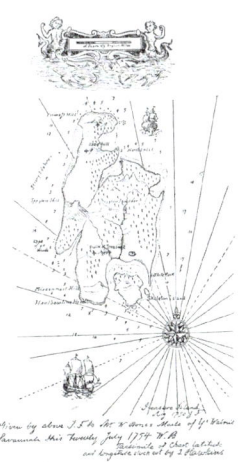

Map of Treasure Island from Robert Louis Stevenson's book *Treasure Island*, 1883

Treasure Island the novel

This adventure novel about pirates and buried gold was first published in 1883. It is full of character, atmosphere and action. It created the popular figure of the 'one-legged pirate with a parrot on his shoulder'. Many ideas from *Treasure Island*, such as the map with a red X to indicate where the treasure is, can still be found in pirate stories even today.

Lost Treasures

Death of Captain James Cook, George Carter, 1783

Captain Cook's Treasure

Captain James Cook (1728 – 1779) was a British explorer and was part of the Royal Navy.
He made three voyages to the Pacific Ocean and was the first European to reach the Hawaiian Islands.
During his third voyage in the Pacific, he was killed in Hawaii in a fight with the natives. Legend says that the natives took everything they could from Captain Cook's ship. They found treasures, guns and lots of personal objects belonging to the crew.
When the King of these natives saw the treasure, he ordered his people to bury it, because he thought these objects had magical powers.
Many people believe that this treasure is buried on the Hawaiian island called Kauai but nobody has found it yet!

Captain Kidd's Treasure

William Kidd (1654–1701) was a Scottish sailor. He was born in Dundee, then moved to New York, where he married a rich English woman. At first he worked with the British Government, but later he was accused of piracy after a voyage in the Indian Ocean. In the end he was executed for this crime, but even today nobody knows for sure if he really was a pirate.
The legend tells the story of Captain Kidd and his crew of pirates. After robbing lots of ships, they decided to go up the Connecticut River in New England USA, to look for a place to bury their stolen gold. They say the treasure is buried on the exact spot where the full moon shines. Three people must form a triangle around this spot and start digging. Lots of people have tried but again, nobody has found it yet!

74

Sunken Ships

The Titanic

Sinking of the Titanic

The most famous ship which ended its voyage in tragedy is the Titanic.

The Titanic, ironically known as the 'unsinkable ship', left from Southampton, England to go to New York. This was its first voyage, but after only four days, it hit an iceberg and sank in the Atlantic Ocean on 15th April 1912.

The ship was now at the bottom of the sea and many people started to look for it. Eventually the wreck of the Titanic was found in 1985, south-east of Mistaken Point in Newfoundland. Since then, divers have brought some objects to the surface. However there are still a lot of objects on the ship and most importantly, they still haven't found the biggest treasure, diamonds! Some people say that two Swiss brothers, who boarded the Titanic in Southampton, had a huge quantity of diamonds equal to about £ 200,000, but since the disaster, nobody has seen them.

The Merchant Royal of Dartmouth

The Merchant Royal of Dartmouth

The Merchant Royal of Dartmouth probably lost one of the biggest treasures of all time at sea.

It was returning to England with Spanish treasure aboard, when there was a terrible storm. It sank on 23rd September 1641, off the coast of Land's End in the south-west of Great Britain.

In the ship's hold there was £300,000 in silver, £100,000 in gold and jewels and hundreds of pearls, diamonds and other precious stones. It also carried lace and spices ready to be sold all over Europe, so many merchants were shocked when they read about the disaster in the newspapers. None of this treasure was ever found or washed ashore.

The Golden Age of Piracy

From Seaman to Pirate

The Golden Age of Piracy was from about 1690 to 1730. Let's look at how seamen became pirates. For years European countries like England, France and Spain were at war. They fought a lot of battles at sea and the governments at that time told their sailors to rob from the ships they captured.

After peace arrived in Europe, the governments didn't want these seamen anymore, but these men didn't know any other kind of job. Therefore they continued to do what they knew - attack and rob ships, this time without the permission of their governments. They were now pirates!

Sea Routes

Map of the West Indies, Antilles, and Caribbean Sea, 1818

During this Golden Age, pirates operated in the Caribbean sea, the sea to the east of America, and the sea off the west coast of Africa. Why was this? Well, there was a lot of trade between Africa and America at that time, so there were lots of ships to attack which were full of all kinds of treasure They didn't only steal treasure, but anything they needed and sometimes even the ship!

They had small fast boats to reach the ships. They often used cannon balls and other weapons to take possession of the ship. In this period, most pirates were English or American and one of the most famous pirates was Blackbeard.

Blackbeard

His real name was Edward Teach and he was born near Bristol in England in 1680. At this time Bristol was a very important city in England because of trade to the American colonies, especially slave trade. He had a very thick black beard which is where his pirate's name comes from. He was so fierce-looking that sailors gave up their ships without a fight. He concentrated on the sea route between the West Indies and the American colonies on the east coast.

Soldiers finally killed him on 22nd November 1718 during battle. Even if he looked fierce, he never harmed the people he captured or robbed.

The End of the Golden Age

About 1830, governments decided to work together to stop piracy. The Jamaican government also helped with their new laws and soon they captured most pirates. Pirates still exist today, but the Golden Age was definitely their most fortunate period in history.

The Jolly Roger

This is the typical flag used by pirates. It is black with a white skull and two long bones in an X form under it. When people saw this flag, they were scared because it was a sign that the pirates were ready to kill if they didn't get what they wanted.

Nowadays it is still used to indicate danger, for example on bottles which contain poison.

Decide if the sentences are True (T) or False (F).

		T	F
	Seamen became pirates after the war ended.	☑	☐
1	The pirates only wanted gold when they attacked a ship.	☐	☐
2	Bristol was an American colony.	☐	☐
3	Blackbeard was very frightened.	☐	☐
4	Blackbeard died while fighting.	☐	☐
5	Governments decided to work with pirates again.	☐	☐

Test Yourself

Choose A, B or C to complete the sentences.

Billy Bones kept the map.
A ☐ in his pocket **B** ☑ in his sea chest **C** ☐ under his bed

1 Many years before .... buried the treasure on the island.
A ☐ Billy Bones **B** ☐ Captain Flint **C** ☐ Ben Gunn

2 Billy Bones died after speaking to ....
A ☐ Long John Silver **B** ☐ Black Dog **C** ☐ Pew

3 Billy Bones was once part of .... crew.
A ☐ Captain Smollett's **B** ☐ Captain Silver's
C ☐ Captain Flint's

4 The ship left for the island from ....
A ☐ London **B** ☐ Liverpool **C** ☐ Bristol

5 At the start of the voyage Long John Silver was the ship's ....
A ☐ cook **B** ☐ cabin boy **C** ☐ captain

6 .... found the buried treasure.
A ☐ The Doctor **B** ☐ Silver **C** ☐ Ben Gunn

7 The name of the British flag is the ....
A ☐ Roger Union **B** ☐ Union Jack **C** ☐ Jolly Jack

8 Captain Smollett broke his arm ....
A ☐ fighting **B** ☐ climbing a tree
C ☐ putting up the flag

9 Israel Hands attacked Jim with a ....
A ☐ gun **B** ☐ knife **C** ☐ bottle

10 At the end of the story, ... pirates were left on the island.
A ☐ two **B** ☐ four **C** ☐ three

Syllabus

Topics
Adventure
Betrayal
Loyalty
Courage
Friendship

Grammar and Structures
Verb tenses: present, past, future
Modals
Question forms
Synonyms / antonyms
Adjectives, comparative and superlative forms
Prepositions
Conjunctions
Pronouns
Quantifiers
Verb patterns

Functions
Discuss plans
Ask for and give information
Give instructions
Make suggestions
Agree / disagree

Teen ELi Readers

Stage 1
Mark Twain, *A Connecticut Yankee in King Arthur's Court*
Maureen Simpson, *In Search of a Missing Friend*
Charles Dickens, *Oliver Twist*

Stage 2
Robert Louis Stevenson, *Treasure Island*
Mary Flagan, *The Egyptian Souvenir*
Mary Flagan, *Val's Diary*
Maria Luisa Banfi, *A Faraway World*
F. H. Burnett, *The Secret Garden*

Stage 3
Charles Dickens, *David Copperfield*
Maureen Simpson, *Destination Karminia*
Anonymous, *Robin Hood*